The/ Forty/ One

The/ Forty/ One

LIFE HACK PRINCIPLES FOR A BETTER YOU

ALEXANDER YANGS

The Forty One

Copyright© 2020 by Alexander Yangs

ISBN: 978-978- 983-909-4

Published by The Execution Shop (TES)

Lagos, Nigeria

Edited by Isime Esene

Cover Design: @omeyispeaks

Contents

Dedication

This book is dedicated to my wife Omeyi, my sons, Farrell and Darren and my entire family for their warmth, guidance, acceptance and consistently believing and standing by me through all my adventures, and for trusting me to lead and share with the world.

Acknowledgements

God, for in whom I put all of my trust and hope and with whom I am. My pastors, mentors and teachers, Kemi Oluyele, Femi Obaweya, Bankole Sadipe, Wale Adenuga, Doyin Oduwole, Kayode Ojo, Segun Lawal, Jide Odusolu, Jumoke Adenowo, Jide Ojo, Kanmi Dasilva, Wale Adefarasin, Tony Rapu and the many people whose lives have inspired me towards greatness in simplicity.

Foreword

Many points.

Delivered straight to the point.

Well, we don't expect less from Alex Yangs. He's a brilliant communication and strategy consultant.

The points etched in THE FORTY ONE cover many aspects of life and living. Some make you smile or laugh. And some will make you go hmmm, and you might even close the book temporarily – to reflect a little bit more.

This is a good book. One you can finish in an Uber ride or that short flight between Lagos and Abuja or New York and Washington.

Alex, thank you for articulating these priceless thoughts.

All who read this will be better.

THE FORTY ONE by Alexander Yangs. Highly recommended.

Wale Adenuga

Preface

I work in the creative media and communication industry, developing solutions to individuals and companies stretched over eighteen years.

In most instances, I find people in sessions or meetings with me taking notes or as with the saying now, 'tweetable quotes' and how these seemingly simple words changed perceptions or brightened the room and recharged the people towards a more meaningful expression in navigating life.

There were only so many meetings I could sit in, and only so many people I could reach or inspire per time. Then came the lockdowns in an attempt to flatten the curve of the spread of COVID-19, a pandemic level crisis which now meant less contact with people or physical meetings. After ninety days of the lockdown which as you can imagine required a lot of adjusting to what the new normal had become birth the idea of capturing some of these quotes in text with deeper insights or context from which they were made. It was exciting but also inspiring, especially since it was happening at a time I was trying to figure out what I wanted to do next, how to do it, and why I needed to do it.

I feel so blessed and proud because more often, little gift seeds are hiding inside of us waiting to sprout amidst seeming storms.

My hope with my first authored book is that its content will inspire greatness towards being a better you.

Introduction

This book is a compilation of quotes and principles that have guided me and the things that continue to shape my mind, lifestyle, and self-expression within my community.

In this book, several principles are touching on relationships, family, business, career, success, failure, religion, community, law, wisdom, and lifestyle. I am always excited to share my experiences, learnings, and sound principles that continue to shape my life to be better while being mindful that principles or ideals are things that are hard to prove whose ideas are right and whose are wrong. You must insert the most positive values to make it real.

1. Success is not a destination; it is a journey you should take with those heading in the same direction

Often we allow the fear of failure to limit our big view of success. Society has conditioned us to believe it is one ultimate thing. But I have come to understand that it is a combination of several small pockets of winning as you travel the path of success despite the failures the journey has installed.

Think about it this way, only a successful sperm that meets with a successful egg that combines to form an embryo carried by a mum who succeeds in delivering a healthy baby who by some special grace went through specially developed care systems on the journey to becoming you. So don't quit on this journey... take it in and keep moving.

2. The profits of failure are the lessons it brings

Failure is an emotion we were never taught to deal with as a part of growth. Growing up we had many people that taught how to be successful and win. How greatness is only attained without failure. Often we were judged, or in most instances, negatively labelled for failing to the point where it became an elephant-sized burden to carry. For some, it hindered them from believing or even trying. Seldom were their lessons on how to understand failure or how to embrace it quickly and take lessons from it as we push to do better and explore further.

Let's say you kick a stone and fall, do you stay down in fear? Crawl on your belly or should you realise your destination won't come closer in an attempt to be fair or understanding of your fall, so you get up and keep moving? In the same way, when we fail, it carries a lesson or two that if quickly embraced, will propel you forward faster towards success. So I urge you to see failure as an opportunity to admit to self, to re-suit, reset, and restart joyfully.

3. Unforgiveness is a disease that plagues the mind and fuels the heart to disconnect from the soul

Holding someone in unforgiveness always resides in the mind based on hurt feelings or a societal narrative that you must have blood for blood, hurt for hurt, and pain for pain. This only disconnects you from what you are: a beautiful soul that thrives in love, joy, peace, and life.

This disconnect usually becomes a constant burden that stops you from fully living your best life.

4. Forgiveness is to reconnect the heart and mind towards healing the soul

Real freedom is when you are at peace with yourself and others. Your soul rejoices, your mind innovates, your heart is joyful, and your life is refreshed with each passing day.

5. Be intentional about being alive; because life is not a dress rehearsal

There are times in life when you wonder and just generally go with the flow, accepting everything life brings your way and telling yourself that one day you will truly live, but never really get to it.

The truth is, we all have fears inside of us which only become limiting when we believe the fear is greater than our ability to create and make an impact despite our fears.

My take is to start small, start today, start now. Start right, but be intentional about living because this is your life.

Find your happiness, laughter, joy, peace and share.

6. Because we are not guaranteed tomorrow, today we will be rock stars all over again

Yes, we should make plans for tomorrow as it is the responsible thing to do. No human can promise you tomorrow or the guarantee of life in it...therefore in that little way you are serving humanity, let it be your best. Do it like a rock star today and after many tomorrows have passed, history will remember your greatness in service and attest to your status as a rock star.

7. If you learn, teach. If you experience, share. If you live, love.

This principle has been the basis, and one of the driving factors of my personality. My understanding of knowledge is with the question: why learn something that I cannot or will not teach? Or go through an experience that its lessons are best shared and not share? Love is more than enough reason to live, and if you are a believer like me, then you must help more people live life with love for all.

8. If your words carry weight, then exercise humility

It's a wise saying that there is power in the words we speak because it can change our being, community, nation, and the world. We must exercise caution to be mindful that with that power should come with the highest levels of humility. Only then can one inspire character and entrench principles to shape a generation to greatness.

9. Your mistakes are not the sum of who you are

The first time you got scolded or reprimanded based on a mistake, you would have found remorse, tears, and that feeling of wanting to do better; but most of all, not wanting to repeat the same. Yes, that exists as part of a humbling fact that your growth leaves lessons for generations to learn. While at different times you felt broken by those mistakes, they prepared you to inspire better for yourself and for others to be lifted, knowing that there is still great (creative) use for a broken vessel. Yes, you made that mistake, did you take its lessons or condemn yourself? That mistake is not the sum of who you are or who you are to be, so pick yourself up and keep moving forward.

10. Safe spaces should be about life; not gender, race, culture or religion

Several situations foster the term "life isn't fair" or leave certain people feeling marginalised. While the concept of safe spaces is laudable, it is self-serving and hypocritical when created on the foundations of biases like gender, race, religious orientation, or culture.

It should be about human life and the diversities of hope.

11. Obtaining selfish desires by violent acts destroy the soul

The desire to pick a blossoming flower will never fade. But understanding allows you to appreciate its beauty with joy, and wisdom teaches you to abstain. No should mean no.

We all must be responsible enough to take care of and protect the weak among us, seek understanding, and embrace wisdom.

12. Time makes the decisions you don't

Thinking about thinking without taking action is a futile endeavour.

Our lives measurements are in units of time. Therefore, we must intentionally and carefully consider every decision we make.

The one thing that we can never have enough of is time, so as leaders, we must become one with making decisions rather than avoiding them.

For success relies on making only the best decisions – and note, that the decisions you don't take, will get made for you.

13. Desire attracts understanding

The first principle of understanding should be desire. Because of this, understanding is made perfect.

Throughout history, the greatest discoveries made were driven by a desire to understand the mysteries around our world. Why do some creatures fly and others don't? How does fire work? What does the earth look like from above? How can we be limitless? The why, the when, the where the who, and the how. The desires posed in these questions are what attract understanding and understanding births more desire to understand more.

14. Don't pretend to be in the ninety-nine; admit to being the one

There are times when we lose sight of faith or self to connect or believe beyond logic. These are the times when the created no longer recognizes the creator and starts walking on a lost path. Like a computer, sometimes gets outdated and needs an update or upgrade. But unlike it, you are still the most valuable.

The problem today is that so many people are lost and need help and guidance back to the right path to grow wholly, but won't admit it because societies narrative gives the impression that it is no longer cool to be the one. So now we must all 'fake' that we are in the ninety-nine, sort of like the lost leading the lost without faith. I take joy knowing that you will be saved by the freely given reckless love of God because you are never truly alone.

15. Sex is to desire or attraction, as intimacy is to truth and care

We all can desire or be attracted to someone or something about someone. But, there is always going to be that struggle for balance between sexual attraction, and intimacy in relationships. I have seen couples sexually attracted to each other yet devoid of intimacy. There are others who thought sex would help them attain intimacy, but after the act, feel more distant and lost. Intimacy is nurtured by the sincerity of heart and selfless care, and so being your true self is what attracts and stirs intimacy in relationships. Find your rhythm in simple conversations and laughter, and intimacy will be its reward.

16. If wealth is power, then the healthy are the most powerful

Fitness and a healthy lifestyle aren't for social, cultural statements or public adoration. It is a personal decision towards attaining power. Yes, the compliments it attracts are refreshing and desirable, yet they are merely natural benefits that follow your effort.

Wealth often confuses people in the difference between eating, living healthy, and the enjoyment of being able to afford anything. I would say everything, but time has shown it is not a sustainable habit for a healthier you.

Exercise and eat healthy for wealth and health are not mutually exclusive, you can attain both.

17. Growth comes with its level of pain

What your mind believes is what will condition your growth.

As we discover and access knowledge, we know more. As we know more, we grow as individuals. But with this growth, comes its level of pain. However, its pain is not to kill or destroy you. It is to help you open a new door to another level of growth.

Social conditioning tells a man he should never show weakness, but a man who understands weakness can find his greatest strength.

18. To live in Christ is to fully acknowledge your rights as a child of God

In Christianity, we are taught to live by faith, start by faith and finish in faith.

To become a son or daughter of God you must accept Christ as the key to your adoption. Therefore, should you continue to live by the laws that shackled you and kept you in darkness? Or, is this because you have compartmentalised your heart and your acceptance of faith is only at a portion of your heart, thereby unable to fully transform your mind?

To live in Christ is to fully acknowledge your rights by faith, start by faith and finish wholly in faith.

19. Creativity enjoys constraint

Being creative is not a function of abundance or having all the right tools at your disposal all the time. Creativity relishes the idea and challenge of nothing — sort of like a blank canvas with odds stacked against the brush, but still, it creates. Beauty is the only thing you can bring forth from ashes when you apply yourself. As on many occasions, I am at my most creative when solving problems in scenarios that are like ashes — with extreme difficulties to fix.

Ask my long-time friend and brother Adebola Williams when his magic touch truly gets activated and he will tell you, it's under constraints.

So what am I saying? Do not be dismayed when you face constraints, it is life's way of helping you develop your creative juices and apply them because we were all made to create.

20. Passion is not a leader to follow

Growing up we hear the saying often that you must follow your passion to be successful. Many lived by this principle and made passion a leader to follow. This led to some awful decision making because passion dictated. I have come to understand that passion isn't the goal but happiness and the excitement to propel you towards it is where passion thrives per time. So you can be amazing at a learned skill, or raw talent and not be passionate about it, but everyone doesn't understand why and sometimes judge you. Do not join in judging yourself harshly for what gives you happiness is what passion will fuel. Passion is not a leader to follow but rather a great self-motivator towards finding happiness.

21. If the one objective is too many objectives, then progress will be stifled

As with the saying that too many cooks spoil the broth when a goal has too many objectives, everyone gets distracted and the energy required is divided into several smaller parts that take away from achieving the goal. Imagine several captains sailing one ship with different opinions on route, wind, and speed? It only just makes the journey complex and tedious to get to, make one objective per time and focus on it.

22. Ask questions and learn with an application mindset

ASK, or Assimilate Simple Knowledge as I would call it, is one of the most difficult things younger generations, especially in the African continent, contend with.

I have found that this is based on fear of not knowing or being slow to learn. There is also the instance where parents raise kids not to "ASK too many questions". But the truth is that complex things are simpler for some to process than others, and the fastest way to grow and catch up is to ask questions to understand till it becomes simple knowledge for you to apply.

23. Poverty isn't a state of mind

There are always going to be poor people amongst us, not necessarily by choice and not the mindset measurement often used by the wealthy…that poor people are lazy and simply need to work harder to escape poverty. The truth is there are circumstances in some climes, economic or religious realities that keep the poor even poorer no matter how hard they work. In Nigeria, if you successfully get a minimum wage paying job which is roughly $78 a month multiplied by 12 months is $936 for a family of one, the basic amenities of food, shelter, and clothing still elude you. Rent is still paid yearly in bulk, so for shelter, one-bed 'self-contained' flat plus all fees approximately take 65% off your yearly wages, maintenance and utilities take up another 12% leaving you with 23% for food, clothing, work commute, training, religious charity, savings and relatives — which is not sufficient.

Poverty is an unclear balance between contentment, exposure and knowledge.

While it is possible that it is caused by a series of bad choices, that in itself is not a totally proven factor.

So next time the government, really wealthy individuals and fancy motivational speakers want to refer to poverty as a 'mindset' that only pushes the poor to heap blame on themselves and feel helpless and hopeless, ask yourself what the actions of your mindsets have done to truly elevate them. What options or safety nets do they have, after all, isn't the true purpose of humanity to serve and help others for the greater good?

24. To believe is to identify with possibilities

While the ideology around faith in something you cannot see, touch, or physically control its outcome is a constant struggle for man, it does not negate the possibility of men getting the expected outcome of faith.

We all grew up knowing the importance of belief, faith, and never doubting, but all are the same and they are all part of who we are: hopeful humans

25. Not all your gifts and talents are for money

First, you must understand what money is by definition: a medium of exchange in the form of coins and banknotes. Some of us have so many skill sets and talents. Some are natural giftings and others are developed by circumstances/opportunities over time. Friends and sometimes family are always cheering you on to start or convert it into a business venture or for-profit, motivational speakers tell you it 'must' be for profit. But I believe otherwise, and I want you to consider a different view. Ask yourself, if all your talents are for money "payment for work" then what will fuel your joy, happiness, and mental health?

I believe that some gifts are fuel for leading a happy life, fostering relationships, and accessing doors, so enjoy them and be refreshed simply because you enjoy being whole.

26. Silence is not golden; it is complicit to every action

No, this is not saying you must be a commentator on all subject matters. While there is a time to speak and a time to listen so you can speak with wisdom, The man who chooses to be silent on everything stands for anything. We must defend the weak, oppressed, assaulted or stifled amongst us lest we be complicit to its actions.

27. Fear hinders, but love fosters the creation

You were not created in fear or worry; for in fear you build up walls, you turn off your lights, and you stop creating. Worry keeps you from doing exploits and stepping out of the shadows of men to create. So, we stay hidden. A friend once told me that the only shadow you should ever be under is that of the almighty God who is wholly embodied in love and by this love, he created a world in his image by which it is sustained.

28. Kindness is not a sport; it is a spirit

There is no medal or recognizable award for 'best in kindness', but its reward is Joy!

So many times you see people trying to televise their show of kindness, shouting on the rooftop about self-gratification for an expression of generosity, or outcompete when there is a watching crowd but withdraw to anger and regret once the crowd isn't cheering.

You are kind simply because there is a kind outpouring spirit, never try to change that.

29. With honesty, integrity and love, a man must guard his name

In a time, long before technological advancement and tools for communicating truth, people were held by their word and in time established their reputation. Your name will go far for exploits good or bad.

Integrity will open doors for trust and your willingness to love despite societal, cultural or religious outlook. As we evolve into the future, most of these values are gradually being lost, therefore we must reflect and restore these lost values individually to make for a lasting positive legacy as a generation, for the sum of a man is his name.

30. It is not the end but a curve when people give up on you

Expect people to be people because just like you, they are not perfect. Everyone is on a journey of self-discovery which means sometimes, their focus will be selfish and they will not be able to hold the high ground you have placed them on.

So it is not the end but a curve when people give up on you. This doesn't make them bad people.

Never give up on yourself for when you do, that is an end.

31. By all means, work smart to be successful

If you live in a world that seeks to identify with success, then by all just means be successful, but do not forget service to your neighbours, your community, and your nation.

A world without service is like a world without seeds.

32. My understanding of women is Patience, Love and Repeat.

There are unspoken rules in a relationship. Sometimes we carry in our minds unspoken expected outcomes from our partner, yet harshly punish them for not being mind readers. Words are the better means of expressing those rules to a man, and getting him to buy in or live by those rules. Unspoken rules in relationships can slowly kill the soul of that relationship, and yes, it is both ways. Use words, be patient, love, and repeat.

33. Wisdom is both a head and a heart journey

The heart is not built for logical reasoning and as such relies on the mind through its lenses of engagement and knowledge with the world for advice. While the mind in all its logical and analytical capacities can learn empathy, it is not its natural disposition. Time has proven that best wisdom is both a head and a heart journey, but its application is instinctively tilted to the heart when logic fails.

34. Imagination breaks the limitations of logic

Logic follows a strict principle of valid, justifiable reasoning. You could say sort of like thinking in a box. For instance, logic sees circles as circles and squares as squares. While imagination sees circles that can fit in squares for stability. We were created to be boundless, to explore and imagine a reality that transcends the norms of culture, race, religion and gender. Imagination sees the universe as a blank canvas to explore. So you can dream, be different, and create.

Your imagination can break the limitations of logic.

35. Love is like a garden and all who engage must tend to it to foster growth

In a love-based relationship there should always be a 100% given but not in the usual share we read where there is the 80/20 or 50/50 or 99/1. In this instance, both parties must give 100%, so that even when one party is unable to access their love base for a while, the relationship is still at 100%. For a beautiful garden is a beautiful garden and the world doesn't care much for who poured most water, it just stays inspired by its beauty.

36. Law is not passionate, it yields to reason and provable facts

Make peace in truth. Indeed, make peace with your neighbour and not let your ego be the enemy. Reconcile with your accuser so you may once again resume a friendly relationship before he hands you over to the judge. For the judge, based on reason and provable facts, can get you incarcerated.

37. To dream, innovate, and take action is to imagine a reality

What is reality? Is it "the state of things as they exist, as opposed to an idealistic or notional idea of them"? Or is it a thing that exists with provable fact having existed only in one's mind and dreams? Reality is a factual action construct born from dreams, innovation and imagination. So, allow yourself to dream and innovate. And more importantly, take action.

38. HOPE – Holding On to Possibilities Everyday

Hopeless people are dead people. With each new day we wake up to uncertainty, a piece of grim news, a hurt, or new joys —never fully understanding if today is the day the universe will align for us but we hope. We can't see it or touch it but we hope. We imagine it, we dream it, and we hold on to possibilities every day. Guard hope and never let its light be stolen.

39. Your personality is not fixed

What is the level of your exposure? What has conditioned you or shaped your personality? It is easy to see why you would believe that this is the only way to being you. Consider your answers to the questions, change your circle and work on your exposure. You will realise that your personality is not fixed, it is an evolving part of self-discovery and enlightenment.

40. Parenting is continuous

Being a parent isn't an automatic certification in great parenting. Like every other subject, it involves learning, re-learning and unlearning. Parenting is the continuous impartation of knowledge to children or wards without a set date for 'graduation'.

41. Your lips, heart, and demeanour must tilt towards gratitude

For gratitude begets more blessings, favour, or goodwill. For with a sincere heart of gratitude seeds planted will grow, expand, and flourish. For truly, no one owes you anything, therefore in everything, we must be thankful.

42. Your business is not a democracy, but a solution to a need

Have you been in that situation in business when it seems like everyone but you know has an idea as to what your business should be doing, and how it should be doing it? You would hear comments like; you should sponsor this. You should branch into that industry. You should not hire more hands. Oh wait, why are you serving that kind of client? Or why don't you just follow what everyone seems to be doing? While there is the place for team input, professional or expert consultation geared towards shaping a business, it is still not a democracy. You made a conscious decision to build a business to fulfil a need so the question is: are you doing that?

43. Life teaches in retrospect

So before you take the next steps, ask yourself: would I be proud of this in three to five years? Do I have enough information to make the right decisions today? For in yesterday lies many lessons. Reflect, grow and don't let ego be the enemy.

Author's Note

We have finally come to the end of this book. Did it give you new insights into the world you live in? Is there a shift in your perception? Did you allow its words to sip through towards the making of a better you?

I feel blessed to have been able to put this together, but I would not have been able to do it if not for friends. Relationships are important for every part of life's journey and incredible things can happen when you tap from its network. For this, I am forever grateful. So, I say thank you to those that helped me launch this book and get its message out to the world.

Soon, I will tell our stories in hope to foster true and supportive friendships amongst many.

To the one who is finding life's journey difficult today, and circumstances seem to be stacked against you finding a better and joyful you, I will leave you with these words.

There is this love I have found that I'll never lose. I'm holding it forever because this love I'll always choose. This love made it all better and gave me a happier ever after. A love that never lets me go and never leaves me low. When all was gloomy, this love pulled me, made it all sunny, with words so warm like milk and honey and I will be foolish not to share this love with you.

This love is God, and in this love comes power and peace. Today, I ask that you take a chance and seek out this love. There is no greater love known or care shown, for there is no dirt that this love won't wash. Every struggle, every pain you have felt doesn't mean you are never going to breathe again, for as the sun shines so will you, and as the moon and stars make the night bright it will lead you right. Remember, stars can't shine without darkness and the skies are dull without stars.

Do not be afraid for this God will uphold you [Isaiah 41:10], lead you to springs of life-giving water, and wipe every tear from your eyes [Revelation 7:17].

Feedback

I would love to hear about how this book has helped you towards being a better you or varying opinions on some of the principles shared here.

Please leave a review on Amazon or you can share your thoughts on Instagram and Twitter and tag me @thealexyangs.

Speaking Engagement

If you are planning a seminar, expert panel discussions, training workshops, company retreats or faith-based dialogues for impact, I am open.

Kindly use any of the following contact details to reach me.

@thealexyangs or +234 (0) 8022226653

Solutions Strategy / Business Consult

If you are kicking off a new project and don't even know how and where to start, struggling with growth hacks, market entry or general communication and marketing strategies that yield results, contact **TES** for a **free,** quick design thinking session. www.tescreates.com or hello@tescreates.com

About the Author

Alexander Yangs is a solutions strategist, founder and CEO of The Execution Shop (TES).

He is former group director, growth at RED | for Africa and CEO Red Media Africa. Trained as a network security engineer and software developer with work experience as a systems tech specialist in the aviation, oil & gas, and shipping sectors for a few years before moving to the creative communication industry.

He has over 18 years of experience in the marketing communication industry which has seen him lead teams, providing ideas and agency solutions to brands across digital, advertising, public relations, market-entry, sales strategy, audio & video content development/production, and crisis management. Alex has worked with top firms including Friesland Campina, Unilever, CFAO, Oando, Access Bank, Vitafoam, Sterling Bank, GTBank, SC Johnson, Airtel, ARM amongst others.

He is also an executive music producer, songwriter, artist broker, and manager, with original music and scores for corporate clients including Coca Cola, Sprite, Fanta, Pepsi, ARM, Virgin, Vitafoam, Sigma Pensions amongst others.

Alex enjoys speaking, music, travel, family time, sports, and movies.

He is a strong believer in the power of Christ, grace, and mercy.

Glossary

Reflect – to think carefully and deeply about something

Ego – your sense of your value and importance

Retrospect– thinking about a past event or situation, often with a different opinion of it from   the one you had at the time

Demeanour – the way that somebody looks or behaves

Flourish – to develop quickly and become successful or common

Imparting – to pass information, knowledge, etc. to other people

Complicit – involved with other people in something wrong or illegal

Enlightenment – knowledge about and understanding of something; the process of understanding something or making somebody understand it

Evolving – to develop gradually, especially from a simple to a more complicated form; to develop something in this way

Grim – unpleasant and depressing

Idealistic – having a strong belief in perfect standards and trying to achieve them, even when this is not realistic

Notional – based on a guess, estimate or theory; not existing in reality

Logic – a way of thinking or explaining something

Principle – a moral rule or a strong belief that influences your actions or law, a rule or theory that something is based on

Validity – the state of being legally or officially acceptable or the state of being logical and true

Justifiable – existing or done for a good reason, and therefore acceptable

Reasoning – the process of thinking about things rationally; opinions and ideas that are based on logical thinking

Tend – to care for somebody/something

Fallible – able to make mistakes or be wrong

Curve – a line or surface that bends gradually; a smooth bend

Embodied – to express or represent an idea or a quality

Fosters – to encourage something to develop

Innate – that you have when you are born

Ideology – a set of beliefs, especially one held by a particular group, that influences the way people behave or a set of ideas that an economic or political system is based on

Resolved – determined

Boundless – without limits; seeming to have no end

transcends – to be or go beyond the usual limits of something

Canvas – a strong heavy rough material used for making tents, sails, etc. and by artists for painting on

Limitations – the act or process of limiting or controlling somebody/something or a rule, fact or condition that limits something

Entrench – to establish something very strongly so that it is very difficult to change

Reconcile – to find an acceptable way of dealing with two or more ideas, needs, etc. that seem to be opposed to each other or to make people become friends again after an argument or disagreement.

www.ingramcontent.com/pod-product-compliance
Lightning Source LLC
Chambersburg PA
CBHW020935160726
47993CB00007B/2796